Prayers from the Flowers

To Donna -
This Christmas which
you have made so
meaningful to me -
I thank you - & say
Love

Prayers from the Flowers

ANN GIRAY

ESSA BOOKS

Printed in the United States of America

Library of Congress Catalogue Card # 98-072425

ISBN 0-9665301-0-1

Published by
ESSA Books
P. O. Box 28337
Atlanta, Georgia 30358-0337

Our doubts are traitors,
And make us lose the good we oft might win
By fearing to attempt.

—William Shakespeare (1564–1616)

Contents

Acknowledgements

The people who through the years have added such richness to my life are now scattered across the world. These friends know who they are and from my heart I thank them. However, some names stand out and should be written here. In England, George Kasabov who taught me much and I remembered him while writing 'The carnation' prayer. Goodie McCann, with all her giving nature and commitment to those lucky enough to cross her path. In Australia, Dr. Stephen Davies for all the wonderful talks we share and his dedication to health of mind, body, and spirit. In Jamaica, Dodie and Ralph Thompson and many others, but specially Mike Henry who generously shared his knowledge of publishing built over the years from his own publishing house in Kingston. In America, Shelley and Judd Marcus, Chuck Leavell, Jim Crisp, Tom Glennon, Kenny Leon, Derek Walcott, all who contributed a lot towards my being granted a green card. Many thanks, too, to Giles O'Neal for all his editorial skill and insight into the work, and William Llopp, my accountant, who, at the right moment, reminded me I was a writer and to get on with it! One friend preferring to remain in the background, has always been there for me, but the background she inhabits is the ground I stand on; dear Essie. Tamar Burchill's talent for loving care in putting this book together speaks for itself. Both love and care are synonymous with her life. All who read John Clive's preface will see the powerful writer he is and the depth of his vision. To be counted in his family of friends is a trust to be honoured with only the best one can do. I try!

And so to my children, one son and two daughters, the three most amazing people I know. It is to you Stephen, Toni-Ann and Corinna, this book is dedicated.

Preface

*T*his is not an age of prayers. In that respect, perhaps more than any other, this age is unique. No culture before ours has been so indifferent to the transcendent. It is not hard to understand. No culture before ours has received such bounty from the exercise of the human mind. Why should mankind invoke the incomprehensible when such unimagined benefits pour forth from the efforts of our own comprehension? Through our own thought and will we have made the blind see, the deaf hear, we have increased the length of our lives, our children live when once they would have died. Through our own thought and will, we have also produced equally unimaginable cruelty and devastation.

It is as though we have found ourselves on a strange, limitless plane; at our feet, stretching to the horizon in all directions, is a carpet of diamonds. But weaving through the astonishing jewels is a plague of scorpions. Our prosperity and our survival seem to depend on our eyes being fixed to the ground. We stand engrossed, trying to distinguish treasures from threats. In the midst of such a landscape how can it be expected that we should lift our gaze and supplicate the heavens?

This is the plane of the intellect. Here the infinite is no more than darkness. It cannot be otherwise, for nothing can exist for the intellect unless it is distinct, that is – unless it is separable from its context. (The word is derived from the Latin *intellegere* "to choose between".)

In prayer, as in love, we temporarily put aside this consciousness of distinctions and separateness. We direct our consciousness instead to the infinite and thus we exercise and experience that aspect of ourselves that is the infinite. To be conscious of this unity is to know peace. Whilst intellectually we may be unable to conceive of peace as anything other than an absence of activity, we have all at least glimpsed the great strength that peace can provide. And here is our experiential evidence that what is nonsense or non-existent to our intellect can have the greatest significance for our deeper understanding.

Today many people are unable to disassociate the idea of prayer from what they perceive as the dogmas of formal religions. And so the need for spiritual communion is denied any expression at all. Such people may find much value and comfort in the following pages. Each prayer is the pure and simple call of a life to its transcendent origins. What can be heard in these beautifully variegated voices is the sound of the mundane affirming its inviolable oneness with the infinite.

John Clive
April 1998

Introduction

*T*here are times when memories of childhood still skid across the forefront of my mind. Seeming to have lost little along the passage of time, they emerge from the vast tank of what once was with an air of acute nowness.

Again I am made to see the child who though still me is surely a me long gone, yet still I see her, knowing what I am is so much of what she once was. Again I step into my grandfather's garden, where my grandmother was only tolerated, listen for the kitchen door to swing shut behind me, and following the paved path I make for the plot of silver birches and from there on to the massed beds of summer flowers bordering the lawn.

Here, just tall enough, I can look full face into a foxglove or from my supposed great height turn my attention downwards, where at my feet pansies scramble about the crowded borders.

In recall it seems in those years it was always summertime and every day the garden a place of heavy scent and sunlit corridors. There, cotton-frocked, I would see the roses and the lilies as playmates and make them the Kings and Queens of my games; the tall evening primrose the prince, and the princess the white delphiniums, my grandmother's favourite.

She loved all white flowers whereas my grandfather couldn't stand them. There was clear evidence of this when cutting the lawn, I walking several steps behind, he mowed the heads off all the daisies along with so many splinters of cut grass. The cruelty of it was almost too much to bear; as fast as I gathered them up for decent burial there were always more flying at me through the air.

Days later, when all was quiet in the kingdom and the grass had grown a little, I would lie on my stomach, put my face among the new sprung daisies and in the only way I knew advise these soon to be beheaded victims 'Not to make a fuss when it comes to bedtime. And say your prayers. And ask God to make you good.'

Church and God were strong topics in my grandparents house, mostly because my grandfather said he didn't believe in any of it and my grandmother insisted that he should.

However, it was only she and I who set off on a Sunday for morning service.

At evening when the twilight crawled across the lawn it was the two of us would sit together, where in a mood to fit the dwindling light below the clock upon the stairs, she began her whisperings of Our Father. Listening I thought how different were these murmurs of hers to those that came from the garden. Out there I had got going quite a choral of voices.

It had, of course, begun with the daisies. Out of their obvious need for quick salvation, in sight of their oncoming slaughter, I had got them at last to follow instructions and say their prayers. But it didn't end there; being a jealous lot, all the others had to join in.

When you think of it, it's not really surprising the first poem I ever wrote as a child was a prayer I over heard from a daisy. Perhaps more surprising is how much time and hard living it's taken to get back to those roots, where, in childlike games of kings and queens and fairy tale princes, I began the long journey towards finding my own way to prayer. And the journey is not yet over, for more and more I find prayer is like love-making, there are so many ways of doing it.

If you who now read this have not found your way to prayer, there is something in the following pages that may work for you. Take one of the prayers, and in it just one little line or even just a word, and for several days take the prayer, or the line, or the word into your life. Repeat it as you drive the highway, reach for a cup of coffee at work, choose an item from off the supermarket shelf, settle down to watch a video, take your toothbrush to clean your teeth.

Every morning say it as you look into the mirror, knowing what you see there is the face of love, your face, that through prayer reflects the Divine. This approach, once started, will bring you to the place where never again will you have to ask yourself, or any other, what is the meaning of life. You will have found it.

Within each one of us are those blessings given when we first came into this life. Blessings which grow-ing into adulthood we often see as contrary to the world we find around us. But the world is a blessing if we can only see it and our Father Mother who are in heaven show us where there is prayer there is no more loneliness.

And it is this that is their eternal gift lit with their love, infused by ours.

Ann Giray
April 1998

The Snowdrop

Even if it seems
I stand so quietly
this white flower
like some snowladen psalm
in stillness sings
praises of You

O Thou!
the source of all song
the lovely One
star above all stars
the sky, the silver sun!
Thou! the whisper in trees
the green sap of things
my life's door, the vein
that runs along the leaf

A bundle of flowers thou art!

O my Father Mother
How I do love Thee!

The Morning Glory

The Morning Glory

In darkness I spring to life
as the sun moves across the sky
to fall from sight
I bloom! I blossom!
Until fading I am seen to die

Encompassing love
Your harvest Lord
is gathered in for purposes
we know not of

Why question this?

Trusting is filled with grace
and learning this where
shall I lift my eyes unless
it be to Your dear face

Much on earth is hidden from us, but to make up for that we have been given a precious mystic sense of our living bond with the other world, with the higher heavenly world, and the roots of our thoughts and feelings are not here but in other worlds.

—Fyodor Dostoevsky (1821-81)

The Cowslip

Looking up, I hear you
Lord of all wonder!
light of my soul!
All across the field
I hear you

In whirl of weather
dew dropping leaves
in insects clatter
bird-whirr of wings
even when busking sunlight
air dusting sheaths
heralds the dark
          night rustling
this flower filled field
in a mingle of voices
lifts too its chorus

And looking I hear you
Lord of all wonder!
light of my soul!
All across the field
I hear you

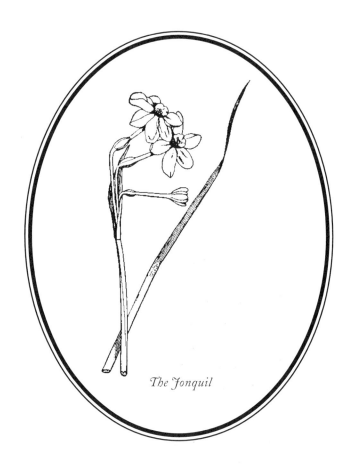

The Jonquil

The Jonquil

In sweet appearance of dawn's glory
in blades of morning
in midday simmer
rain's spatter
sun's glitter
in petalled trumpet

In this garden's afternoon

In twilight swallows hurrying
across day stilled grass
dappled shadowing

In tones of evening
dark discovering

In all time
and for all things
my prayer is
praise Him!
praise Him!

Turn I my looks unto the skies,
Love with his arrows wounds my eyes:
If so I gaze upon the ground
Love then in every flower is found

—Thomas Lodge, (1558–1625)

The Bluebell

Dear Lord
my sash of blue
slips through the wood
in praise of You!

This blue this haze
this trail of bloom
is all in all
in praise of You!

In such Divinity
springs Your dear grace
with You in all
for all love's sake

The Daisy

The Daisy

This bright heart
from where white petals spring
offers the sweetest memories
Your face Lord in all things

Accepting all
loved by all
for what should I pray?

I stand a small flower
Your flower Lord
in every way

The Dogwood

Dear Lord
Father Mother of all
how sweet is spring!
Your stream of life
its promise misting trees

On such a day as this
let me give thanks
for all that is

For You fashioned me right
You fashioned me strong
to bloom as Your vessel
my burden Your song

The Rose

The Rose

Dear Lord of all
have You seen how
here along my stem
You have set thorns?
Even my leaves
are often prickly

I am a mess!

Dear Lord of all
is this Your will
Your secret blessing
to have this thorny stem
push the bud
reminiscent
in amaze of glory
to a flowered beauty
of heavenly grace

All now are striving, every field
Full hymns doth yield
The whole Creation shakes off night
And for they shadow looks the light;

—Henry Vaughan (1622–1695)

The Lily of the Valley

Dear Lord I know well
how You are somewhere near
yet still You keep out of sight
out of hearing

If this is the time for bells?

Down go my roots
up goes my stem
split open shoots
green as a gem
let me unfold
this flower of mine
that I may not hinder
our dear Lord's design

See me O Lord!
O Lord see me!
See how I bloom
and blossom for thee!

The Orchid

The Orchid

As morning dew singles
each blade of grass
so may my voice give sparkle
along this wooden path.
For all of prayer
unveils all nature's song
all verdant green
the light, the spotted dark

Above the leaf
beyond the stem
my petals curl
to flower with grace.
In praise of song
or risk of pain
what's there of meaning
in all of this unless?

Unless
turning again
I lift my voice
to call Your name

The Carnation

How may a stone be made to move
unless
How may the flower be made to sing
unless
How may the cloud tumble
the tide be still?
How may the tears cease?
How may the silent word
be said?

Dear Lord of all
there is small delight
in all this ponderance!

Let me then be struck
by the imponderable!

Love
strikes at the door?

The Iris

The Iris

In taverns of darkness
I stand and wait
in dense deep dark
more dark than day's shade.
All of life's turmoil
its twist and trade
leaves me a tight bud
stiff and afraid.
How may I now
drawn to this hell
open one petal in grace?

How may I once more be
Your own thoughts flowering?

Sweet Lord of all
is this true
how on an instant
seeking you
can all be changed?

In tongues of blue
unsealing, the bud
unfurls its bloom
and all's at peace
and all is You

All things by a law divine
in each other's being mingle.

—Percy Bysshe Shelley (1792–1822)

The Meadow Sweet

Closer to birdsong closer to Your song
dear Lord I spread my lacey bracts
for honeysuckled bees. White slipped
summer flowering, in this hedgerow
I stand sentinel!

Heavy duty this!

Below in the long grass at my feet
grow smaller flowers small as a bird's beak!
Differences they say make the world complete
and I know my place! Or thought I did!

As once more looking down
at those small flowers, it slips
across my thoughts, (Your thoughts
dear Lord?) how really we are all
so very much the same

And all of a sudden
such sweetness hits my face
until my heart in praise sings out
Am I not you? A part of you?
Am I not you for ever and ever
Amen

The Foxglove

The Foxglove

I have to say
sometimes I am sick of speckles
this gangly stalk
hung down with petals
to say nothing of these bees
up my nostrils!
In all this agitation
how can I pray?

My flowers rattle like shells!

Dear Lord
Let me stand here at peace
with the peonies, where afternoon
crawls across the grass
and I can know what quiet is!

But here's the wind
to shake at my lockets
every flower set to chime

Until the breeze settles
a bird whistles
and all of a sudden
it's prayer time!

There is naught else but
'The one eternal Life'
and
'Love' for
the one eternal Life

—S.E.

The Four O'clock

 Thou
father mother of all
as daylight turns to starlight
I am your lamp of flowers.
How may I serve you
through this night?

Hope is the incandescence
of all prayer

And these petals
reflecting this, my prayer
ask that I point the way
through the dark lit garden
and in sight of Your love
ease the way clear

The Water Lily

The Water Lily

Ọ! Thou!
Heart of the lake
heart of the earth
heart of the sky
heart of all fire
eternal flame

May your desire
be in this flower
now for this moment
and all the days
of my life

The Sunflower

Hail! Hail to Thee
O wondrous One!
Hail! Hail to Thee
great light of heaven!
Now may my soaring heart
reflect Your glory

Now may this flower
chime the homespun pasture
with mystic melody

Hail! Hail to Thee
O holy One!
Hail to Thee
flame of my spirit
my lamp, my limb
my breath, my path
See! I am here!
Lead Thou me on

The Passion Flower

The Passion Flower

 Thou!
Who art above and within
our Father Mother
light of heaven
light of the earth
light of my heart

O Thou who art
the giver of blessings
bless me! – that I may become
Thy true disciple

We walked in so pure and bright a light, gilding the withered grass and leaves, so softly and serenely bright, I thought I had never bathed in such a golden flood, without a ripple or a murmur to it. The west side of every wood and rising ground gleamed like the boundary of Elysium, and the sun on our backs seemed like a gentle herdsman driving us home at evening

—Henry David Thoreau (1817-62)

The Evening Primrose

Dear One
Lord of my life
may this flower
always look
heavenwards

In Your glance
through the twilight
let this face
neither look back
or sideways
but turn willingly
to the night
to the power of grace
and Your knowing love
shewn new each day

The Mythical Lotus

The Mythical Lotus

 Thou!
Giver of blessings
light now
the lamp of my heart
that I, ever insightful
of purity and peace
may carry this
through the world
until You bring me home
to rest

Ancient Floral Vocabulary

Absinth	*The Bitterness and Torments of Love*
Acacia	*Love, pure and platonic*
Acanthus	*Love of Fine Arts*
Althea	*Exquisite Sweetness*
Amaranth	*Fidelity and Constancy*
Anemone	*Abandonment*
Angelica	*Gentle Melancholy*
Argentine	*Ingenuity*
Aster	*Elegance*
Basil	*Poverty*
Betony	*Emotion and Surprise*
Bindweed	*Coquetry*
Bluet	*Clearness and Light*
Box	*Firmness and Stoicism*
Bramble	*Injustice and Envy*
Burdock	*Importunity*
Buttercup	*Sarcasm*
Calendula	*Anxiety*
Camellia	*Constancy and Steadfastness*
Carrot	*Good Character*
Cinquefoil	*Maternal Love*
Colchicum	*Bad Character*
Cypress	*Mourning and Grief*
Dahlia	*Sterile Abundance*
Daisy (Easter)	*Candour and Innocence*
Dandelion	*Oracle*
Darnel	*Vice*
Digitalis	*Work*
Dittany	*Discretion*
Elder	*Humility*
Ephemeris	*Transient Happiness*
Everlasting Flower	*Constancy*
Fennel	*Merit*
Fern	*Confidence*
Forget-me-not	*Faithful Remembrance*
Foxglove	*Adulation*
Fuchsia	*Amiability*
Fumitory	*Hatred*
Geranium	*Folly*
Hawthorn	*Sweet Hope*
Heliotrope	*Eternal Love*
Hellebore	*Wit*
Hemlock	*Perfidy*
Holly	*Defence*
Honeysuckle	*Bond of Affection*
Hyacinth	*Amenity*
Hydrangea	*Coldness*
Iris	*Indifference*
Ivy	*Attachment*
Jasmine	*Amiability*
Jonquil	*Amorous Languor*
Jujube-tree	*Relief*
Larkspur	*Open Heart*
Laurel	*Victory and Glory*
Lavender	*Silence*
Lilac	*First Troubles of Love*
Lily	*Purity and Majesty*
Maidenhair	*Bond of Love*
Majoram	*Consolation*
Marvel of Peru	*Flame of Love*
Mallow	*Maternal Tenderness*

Mint	*Wisdom and Virtue*
Milfoil	*Cure and Recovery*
Moonwort	*Bad Payment*
Myrtle	*Love*
Narcissus	*Self-esteem and Fatuity*
Nettle	*Cruelty*
Olive	*Peace*
Orange-tree	*Virginity, Generosity*
Peony	*Shame*
Periwinkle	*Unalterable Friendship*
Pineapple	*Perfection*
Pink	*Pure and Ardent Love*
Poppy	*Sleep*
Privet	*Youth*
Rose	*Beauty and Love*
Rosemary	*Power of Re-kindling extinct Energy*

Rue	*Fecundity of Fields*
Sage	*Esteem*
Sensitive-plant	*Modesty*
Solanum	*Prodigality*
Spindle-tree	*Ineffaceable Memory*
Strawberry	*Intoxication, Delight*
Thyme	*Spontaneous Emotion*
Trefoil	*Uncertainty*
Tulip	*Grandeur*
Valerian	*Read*
Vervain	*Pure Affection*
Viburnum	*Coolness*
Violet	*Modesty*